STAR BY STAR

Star by Star

POEMS

by

Naomi Long Madgett

1965

HARLO PRESS, DETROIT, MICH.

Second Edition

Manufactured in the United States of America by
Harlo Press, 16721 Hamilton Avenue, Detroit, Michigan 48203

Price $1.95

Copies of this book may be ordered directly from the author at
18080 Santa Barbara Drive, Detroit, Michigan 48221

ACKNOWLEDGMENTS

Many of the poems in this collection have appeared previously in the following anthologies and magazines: *The Poetry of the Negro, 1746-1949* (edited by Langston Hughes and Arna Bontemps, Doubleday, 1949); *American Literature by Negro Authors* (edited by Herman Dreer, Macmillan, 1950); *Beyond the Blues* (edited by Rosey E. Pool, Kent, England, Hand and Flower Press, 1962); *New Negro Poets: U.S.A.* (edited by Langston Hughes, Indiana University Press, 1964); *Ik Ben de Nieuwe Neger* (edited by Rosey E. Pool, The Netherlands, Bert Bakker, 1965); *Success in Language/A* (edited by Ethel Tincher, Frank Ross, Shirley Reynolds, and Edward Simpkins, Follett, 1965); *Freedomways; Phylon; The Negro History Bulletin; Negro Digest;* and *Blue River Poetry Magazine.*

A few of the poems in this collection were included in *One and the Many* in 1956.

Some of the earlier selections were first published under the names Naomi Cornelia Long or Naomi Long Witherspoon.

Other books by Naomi Long Madgett

SONGS TO A PHANTOM NIGHTINGALE

ONE AND THE MANY

For my parents

MAUDE AND CLARENCE LONG

and my daughter

JILL WITHERSPOON

CONTENTS

STAR BY STAR

QUEST

I will track you down the years,
　　Down the night,
Till my anguish falls away,
　　Star by star,
And my heart spreads flaming wings
　　Where you are.

I will find you, never fear—
　　Make you mine.
Think that you have bound me fast
　　To the earth?
I will rise to sing you yet,
　　Song of mirth.

I will let you think you won,
　　Perfect dream,
Till I creep from dark and toil
　　To your side,
Hold you to my heart and sleep,
　　Satisfied.

I will track you down the sky,
　　Down the blue,
Till my song becomes the sun
　　Of the years
And the golden April rains
　　Are my tears.

HOMAGE

Consider the eternal Cat,
Bird-watcher supreme,
Who alone among the fluttering things
Waits and is sure.
Incapable of flight and yet secure,
He knows it isn't wings
One needs to soar (or to redeem
The rabbit from the hat).

Their doom foreshadowed when he sees a feather fall,
He knows they do not know
Salvation is the *use* of idle things
Like songs and wings
They think they owe
To time and trust and the redemptive All.

BEGINNING AND END

Spring's earliest suggestion was
A curling, stretching rope of slime
Regurgitated by a morning-sick earth.
And I wondered if all birth begins
With the throwing up of worms.

When all the lies are told, the persevering truth
Will ooze triumphant to the surface of decay.
All life and death is worms
As the tunnels through dead brains will testify.

MORTALITY

This is the surest death
Of all the deaths I know.
The one that halts the breath,
The one that falls with snow
Are nothing but a peace
Before the second zone.
For Aprils never cease
To resurrect their own,
And in my very veins
Flows blood as old as Eve.
The smallest cell contains
Its privileged reprieve.
But vultures recognize
This single mortal thing
And watch with hungry eyes
When hope starts staggering.

ENCOUNTER

What business have these grizzled faces
Now with those flown breezes?
What right have withered lips to poison
Such tender leaves with putrid whisper of remembrance?

No, it is not Jack or Bob or William. Such gentle names
Should not be hurled against the wind and broken.
That dark coat flapping through the shadows
Is no one that you used to know
And no one that it ever was before.

AFTER

The doves are in the eaves
Flapping their eager wings
To go.
Oh, pity the last lonely birds
That fly into the setting sun.

Shadows of their wings
Fall in purple sadness
On the cooling sod.
Pity the last birds
After the flock has flown.

The doves are flapping impatient wings—
The late birds flying alone
And cooing a farewell
That is forever goodbye.
Oh, pity the last, still-later birds
Who have no wings—
Who may only walk in the cold shadows
Alone, alone in the night.

NATIVE

Down the unspun swerve of trackless weeds
I travel unaware,
Propelled by sudden vengeances of seeds
Of anywhere
Whose hues I never learned nor whose design.
Unmindful of intent,
I wander where the knowing roots entwine
The innocent,
And suck the pungent juice into my vein,
And do not question why.
Expect no definition to explain
Or deify.
For blessed or damned, inherent in my lust
And native to my need
Is this same potent urgency that dust
Conveys to seed.

OF SLEEP

This is one way to die: to bury hours
In gray unconsciousness; to blot the sun
From sight, the birds from sound, the roses
From the sickening awareness of too heavy fragrance.
Here is oblivion between the sheeted
Coolness of a shaded tomb.
For one minute eternity to lie unknown,
Unknowing beneath the deepening
    layers of
        forgetfulness.

WOMAN WITH FLOWER

I wouldn't coax the plant if I were you.
Such watchful nurturing may do it harm.
Let the soil rest from so much digging
And wait until it's dry before you water it.
The leaf's inclined to find its own direction;
Give it a chance to seek the sunlight for itself.

Much growth is stunted by too careful prodding,
Too eager tenderness.
The things we love we have to learn to leave alone.

THE RECKONING

The This of that and the That of this
And eventually, finally, all-conclusively the This of this
Must be reviewed and dealt with and made sky-blue clear.
For birth was but a breath ago
Since the last weary dream
Curled up its edges in its newly-dug
Six hearts of clay forgetfulness.
And since the heat and cold and livingness and black decay
Are mint-bright and untold,
And since the burial must be forgot
And the overstatement understated:
The This of that (and unavoidably the This of this)
Must be made plain,
And why and how and what, and sometimes even if.

OUT OF A HEAVEN

Out of a heaven fools devise,
My falling star is flung
To earth's cold crater.
With what hurt dismay
This nothing-sphere that could have been
The world (bright, round enough
To circle all my strength)
Totters on the edge of certain doom!

The bubble breaks, a fluff upon the wind,
A wasted potency poured on a sterile seed
By a willing dream caught naked
In a hostile bed.

DESTINY

How near we are to paradise
Fate does not deign to tell,
Or what direction peril leads
The descent into hell.

Or whether spring's capricious breath
Blows promise to the sun
Or flings away a sterile seed
To earth's oblivion.

By what improbable design
The grasses part our way,
The brooding stars of destiny
Have never stooped to say.

POOR REYNALDO

Reynaldo's dead and gone wherever people go
Who never loved a song.

If he's in heaven, then it must be hell for him,
For it is surely
Vast, high-vaulted halls echoing
Unearthly melody;
And if in hell, —
Why, even hell, especially hell, must have
Its music of a sort.
For tortured souls have ever lifted up a plea,
A prayer, an exaltation of despair
(Not the bright, lilting notes of birds
But deeper and more turbulent)
In song.

His journey here was breath without a sigh,
Words without music,
Shapes without design
Or color.
Where could he go? Where can he be?

Poor, poor Reynaldo,
Dead and still unresting!

NIGHT RIDER

Fling down the night's imperious delay,
Forestall the moth with star-singed wing,
The hovering dark command.
It is but cloud of foam and mist
That rides the red rim down.
Black crow, red doom, and stark of dawn
Will stable him again.

WHITE CROSS

Never mind if dawns refuse to waken you
Though the hills are sleepy-blue with mist;
Never weep if lovers have forsaken you,
Seeming to forget the lips they kissed.

Heavy feet may thoughtlessly tramp over you
Never caring that you had to die;
Silver wings of war may not discover you:
Many are the crosses where you lie.

But when time is lying in the sod with you
And the stillness is its silenced drum,
There'll be one to seek the face of God with you.
Wait for me, my dear, and I will come.

REFUGE

The endless fog winds
Down a gray eternity
As quiet as death.

Shaggy brows brooding,
A deserted house keeps watch
With its blinded eyes.

Hide me, leaves of trees,
Roofs of houses; O hide me,
Secret veils of night.

Fear-removed to shores
Not of my seeking, I find
Harbors that are home.

SONG FOR A SEASON

Through winter's chill, stay warm.
Through blast of wind, keep steady and secure.
December holds no threat this year, no harm
To one protected lovingly. Endure

As seeds endure beneath earth's vigilance.
Some little wisp of dreams is all we know
Perhaps of sun and green and sustenance
Amid the frost and snow.

But this sufficiency
I offer you for balm: that love and dreams
Are life's most tangible reality;
It's time alone that *seems*.

TRINITY: A DREAM SEQUENCE

1.

I will sing you songs until your heart can hear
Their silences,
Shine my lamp until your eyes perceive
The dark from which it springs.

Through the entangled forest of my dreams
Your dream will falter toward me,
And some day we shall meet.

2.

I know you have to find me in your dreaming.
You could not enter mine with so much ease
If the paths were unfamiliar to your feet.

You have to wake and find me lingering,
Some wisp of misty memory
Not completely lost.

(If not, why do you come uncalled into my sleep,
Your voice quieting howling winds,
Your fingers' touch lighting up stars?)

So must the fog lift over waking valleys
Until one day in consciousness you call my name.

3.

Already I have forgotten the phrase
That rocketed to mind. It escapes me
Like a dream untold until too late.

Now I labor over words, trying to capture
Mountains of somewhere: towering out of mist and haze,
Power and height and granite roadways to infinity.

I would give you the song if I could remember,
If I could only recall what star exploded in my dream.

4.

You would not recognize yourself if I should tell you
What truth emerges from your levity and mirth.
Your depth is so disguised that even you
Would be surprised to see your image in the glass
I hold. But let it be;
Enough that I discover you
Over and over, dream and dream again,
In each encounter, and I have a secret
I cannot tell you.

5.
(Morning Song)

I give you love and joy and all good things
That summer brings:
Leaf in a sympathetic breeze, a dawn
To wish upon,

Cool grasses' dew, benevolence of rain,
Release from pain,
Burst of a blossom, sustenance of prayer,
The sun's first flare.

First breath of dawn, the sky's first blue I bring,
A song to sing,
And peace beside a slow and sinuous stream
Where you can dream.

My days' first thought, my nights' last consciousness,
My dreamed caress,
Rebirth of joy and love each day anew—
These are for you.

6.

You walk a highway where pale lilies blow
In the white glare of noon
Breathing cold purity
In approved scentlessness.

Come to the garden; I am not ashamed
To call you.

Shadows of Eden beckon you to musk
Of warm, forbidden roses,
Dark, scarlet petals of discovery.

Come and unmask the secret face of night.
In fragrant fields find truth so bold
And so magnificent that jealous gods
Would name it sacrilege to walk therein.

7.
(Commandment)

The tablet shattered when you touched my hand.
God may have winced,
But I am not convinced
He did. No vision of a Promised Land

Ever evoked such joy. If law opposes
A sin so fair,
Then I will gladly bear
The ancient punishment that humbled Moses.

8.

I will be your Eve,
Fulfill your need of conscience for a name
To call temptation by
And thereby give you peace.

Brand this I give you Apple of Destruction,
Lure of the Golden Death;
It may be so.

But oh, before we trail the long descent,
Driven from paradise, into despair,
Reach out and share my joy.
It well may be
The flame we stretch our longing toward
Is not perdition only but a star.

9.

Was it really you all the time?
You who first stumbled upon me
Behind some sea-soaked rock?
Or was it I who, first surprised to find you there,
Came running then through the salt wind,
Feet wet, hair flying?

Who opened the door?
Who entered first and which one followed?
Out of breath, out of mind, I woke
In the house somebody built of crusted sand.
(To trap us or to give us peace, or both?)
I never knew but thought I knew *I* built it
And led you there.
Was it you?

10.

I will not betray you; do not be afraid
My eyes will tell the secret never told
By word or touch—that you have come to me
In Time, walked with me through rich meadows,
Made revelations on hilltops in the sunlate afternoon
Till shadows fell to cover us in Eden.

Now I will pass alone through milleniums of silence
Before I tell philosopher or sage
Who stands upright at the center of the universe.

11.

Thine is the kingdom of the fervent stars
And gilded dreams
Of silver-singing night.

Thine is the power of the surging wind
To clear the web
Of darkness from my birth.

Thine is the glory of the limitless,
The far-borne hope
Of all my upward flight.

Forever be thy face my loveliness,
Thy hands the wings
That lift me from the earth.

12.
(Trinity)

Of the Father and the father and the son
You are most glorious and noble
And most needful (lover, too, made one).

Of the water and the fire and the blood,
Most cleansed and sacrificial,
Baptized and drowned and still borne breathing
      by the flood.

Of the wine and the plea and the prayer
And the hill hard travelled, climbed in pain,
And the garden known alone in despair;

Trinity in burden, acquiescence, suffering,
Flame and lily and denial of the will,
Joy and sadness and the hopelessness to sing;

Of the spirit and the flower and the dew
You are most You.

13.

I kissed your feet,
Poured fragrant oil upon their weariness
And dried them with my hair.

You did not care
That I had sinned but blessed me

And you were blessed in turn,
Raised to most high potential
By my adoration.

14.

Mine were the arms shielding your infancy.
I dipped you in the Styx, yet left you vulnerable;
Cradled your weakness, sought to ease your sighs
To no avail.

(I was Jocasta, too,
Played to an unsuspecting Oedipus.)

I was the woman you gave up to John.
I watched you crucified,
Saw your head drop in final-seeming death
And wept.

15.

If you should die
I would resurrect you
From stone-locked sepulcher.
From your discarded raiment
I would raise such triumph to the sky
Of truth and wonder
As would rock some universe
Unknown to this.

16.

All love is God, all love
is everything,
eternal drama all-
encompassing.

17.

I tottered on the rim of consciousness
Watching with fretful eyes the hours stage
Their jumbled drama. I sobbed out
Your name and waited for your voice
To drown me in its tenderness.

What dream did you nestle in?
What peace pillowed your head
And muffled the sound of my calling?

A bell's insistence jangled the day awake,
But I am still afraid.

18.

Stark day corrodes the silver of the dream
A little, yes.
And caution insulates gloved fingers now
Against enchantment of a certain touch.
But the splendor does not vanish
Because you avert your eyes
Nor the music cease to shiver
Because your words are quick and cold.

I had to tell you.
Turn away if you must; I always knew
That you would have to turn away.

Still I can sing you songs
In silence more eloquent
Than hope or triumph.

19.

These days I gave to you,
These heights I soared:

Wept but was brave for you—
Suffered, adored—
Made and created you
Out of my need;
Love that awaited you
Nurtured the seed.

Wonder of miracle
Circled your face,
Magical, lyrical
Creature of grace.
Time stopped and stayed for you.
Reverent, proud
Infidels prayed for you,
Saw you and bowed:

Glorious trinity
Fashioned of air!

So much divinity
Man could not bear;
So it is earth for you,

Temporal god,—
Mortal rebirth for you
Straight from the sod.

I shall not weep for you,
Sorrow or smile,
Reach out in sleep for you
(After a while).
What sins they say of us,
Ours be the cost.
Then let them pray for us,
Pardoned, but lost.

SPRING RAINS IN A DREAM

Spring rains in a dream came slipping
over my eyelids.
It was four a.m.
when I opened the window.

I had been ill that day.
Perhaps it was the drugs
that broke the fever of forgetfulness,
releasing scarlet pain: your April face
that last morning
when I couldn't tell if you were crying.

Then I remembered I had dreamed about you.
It was a still life: green stalk on a
        chequered tablecloth
without buds or promise even
of knotty undergrowth predictable of being.
But the stalk was green,
and I knew it was you I dreamed about.

AUTUMN PRELUDE

I dread the falling of the leaves:
    I loved them so in russet years,
    I must not tarnish them with tears
While a torn forest grieves.

I cannot watch the year's decay
    Who once, with faith in spring's rebirth,
    Spilled love upon the dying earth
Where hope's quicksilver lay.

Before October's virgin bride
    (The full moon that must also wane)
    Bleeds where my blood has left its stain,
I think I will have died.

STAR JOURNEY

Alone I tiptoe through the stars,
Precipitously steep,
Watchful lest I wake the gods
And angels from their sleep.

Alone I climb the secret hills
Unknown to mortal feet
And stand upon a peak where you
And I can never meet.

To you who do not dream, I am
A gently tilted head,
A voice that chatters, earth-aware,
A gay mouth painted red.

Better that you possess a cold
Impenetrable stone
Than woo my body while my soul
Tips through the stars alone.

POST-SCRIPT

Still let me find your guarded eyes
As deep with longing as before,
Your hand as warm, though lips and thighs
    Consent no more.

Though passion was our only prize,
Our only region to explore,
What pain it is to realize
    You meant no more!

Recite again those easy lies
Of dreams that night seemed fated for;
Then leave me to my secret sighs,
    Content no more.

THE RACE QUESTION
(For one whose fame depends on keeping
The Problem a problem)

Would it please you if I strung my tears
In pearls for you to wear?
Would you like a gift of my hands' endless beating
Against old bars?

This time I can forget my Otherness,
Silence my drums of discontent awhile
And listen to the stars.

Wait in the shadows if you choose.
Stand alert to catch
The thunder and first sprinkle of unrest
Your insufficiency demands,
But you will find no comfort.
I will not feed your hunger with my blood
Nor crown your nakedness
With jewels of my elegant pain.

TREE OF HEAVEN

I will live.
The ax's angry edge against my trunk
Cannot deny me. Though I thunder down
To lie prostrate among exalted grasses
That do not mourn me,
I will rise.

I will grow:
Persistent roots deep-burrowed in the earth
Avenge my fall. Tentacles will shoot out swiftly
In all directions, stubborn leaves explode their force
Into the sun.
I will thrive.

Curse of the orchard,
Blemish on the land's fair countenance,
I have grown strong for strength denied, for struggle
In hostile woods. I keep alive by being the troublesome,
Indestructible
Stinkweed of truth.

NOCTURNE

See how dark the night settles on my face,
How deep the rivers of my soul
Flow imperturbable and strong.

Rhythms of unremembered jungles
Pulse through the untamed shadows of my song,
And my cry is the dusky accent of secret midnight birds.

Above the sable valleys of my sorrow
My swarthy hands have fashioned
Pyramids of virgin joy.

See how tenderly God pulls His blanket of blackness
              over the earth.
You think I am not beautiful?
You lie!

FOR A CHILD

If only the day need not come when I must tell you,
When you stand on tiptoe looking curiously in the mirror
And ask, "Mommy, am I black?"

If only you need not learn the cruel lesson generations old
And let it cool your gaiety, first a frown creeping between
                   your eyes,
Then your loud and careless voice becoming more and more
                   subdued
Till grimness settles dust on everything you do and say.

If only the day need not come when people stop me on the
                   street and say,
"Now that she's growing up, Bessie,
She looks just like you."

PAVLOV

Unless you remind me,
Unless you ring the bell,
I might forget the hang-dog, mad-dog
Militant response,
Mightn't I?

Is it this that makes you stand
A distance off
Afraid,
Because you find me dangerously
Independently
Passive?

VIOLET

Violet was beautiful at four
In spite of squirming on a wicker stool
As comb teeth snarled her hair,
In spite of yelping with each brush's stroke
Till three fat braids bounced in uncontrolled
Black cotton softness when she ran to play.

Home was the world within the picket fence
And joy, the mottled dog that romped and squealed
With never-questioning delight whenever the door opened.
Here the blue-jeaned princess, with storybook certainty
And power, invented daily paradise. With dandelion-laurel
Would crown unwilling puppy King,
Scold a naughty doll for spilling sunshine,
Or convert an empty box to castle tower.
Then, in bushy-haired elegance,
Mischief flecking dark brown eyes with gold,
She would admire the miracle of her own face's smooth
Black satin sheen, reflected in a magic pool of rain.
Violet at four knew just how beautiful she was.

Violet has started school since then, and things have changed.
Even the dog has noticed, is a little wiser. More cautious
Than he used to be, he holds in check his joy at her return,
First sniffs the air to sense her mood before he flops
His tail. He tries to visualize
What three-horned dragon out beyond the gate
Has touched the proud black princess with unlucky wand
Of ugliness, and cursed her thick-haired beauty
With a sense of shame.

ALABAMA CENTENNIAL

They said, "Wait." Well, I waited.
For a hundred years I waited
In cotton fields, kitchens, balconies,
In bread lines, at back doors, on chain gangs,
In stinking "colored" toilets
And crowded ghettos,
Outside of schools and voting booths.
And some said, "Later."
And some said, "Never!"

Then a new wind blew, and a new voice
Rode its wings with quiet urgency,
Strong, determined, sure.
"No," it said. "Not 'never,' not 'later,'
Not even 'soon.'
Now.
Walk!"

And other voices echoed the freedom words,
"Walk together, children don't get weary,"
Whispered them, sang them, prayed them, shouted them.
"Walk!"
And I walked the streets of Montgomery
Until a link in the chain of patient acquiescence broke.

Then again: Sit down!
And I sat down at the counters of Greensboro.
Ride! And I rode the bus for freedom.
Kneel! And I went down on my knees in prayer and faith.
March! And I'll march until the last chain falls
Singing, "We shall overcome."

Not all the dogs and hoses in Birmingham
Nor all the clubs and guns in Selma
Can turn this tide.
Not all the jails can hold these young black faces
From their destiny of manhood,
Of equality, of dignity,
Of the American Dream
A hundred years past due.
Now!

HER STORY

They gave me the wrong name, in the first place.
They named me Grace and waited for a light and agile dancer.
But some trick of the genes mixed me up
And instead I turned out big and black and burly.

In the second place, I fashioned the wrong dreams.
I wanted to dress like Juliet and act
Before applauding audiences on Broadway.
I learned more about Shakespeare than he knew about
    himself.
But of course, all that was impossible.
"Talent, yes," they would tell me,
"But an actress has to look the part."
So I ended up waiting on tables in Harlem
And hearing uncouth men yell at me:
"Hey, momma, you can cancel that hamburger
And come on up to 102."

In the third place, I tried the wrong solution.
The stuff I drank made me deathly sick
And someone called a doctor.
Next time I'll try a gun.

MIDWAY

I've come this far to freedom and I won't turn back.
I'm climbing to the highway from my old dirt track.
    I'm coming and I'm going
    And I'm stretching and I'm growing
And I'll reap what I've been sowing or my skin's not black.

I've prayed and slaved and waited and I've sung my song.
You've bled me and you've starved me but I've still grown
    strong.
    You've lashed me and you've treed me
    And you've everything but freed me
But in time you'll know you need me and it won't be long.

I've seen the daylight breaking high above the bough.
I've found my destination and I've made my vow;
    So whether you abhor me
    Or deride me or ignore me,
Mighty mountains loom before me and I won't stop now.

NOTE: I have included "Midway," not for its dubious literary merit,
but because of general popular demand. This poem, which I wrote in
1959, has been reproduced without permission, misquoted, and even
published anonymously since its first legitimate appearance in print in
1961. This is the original, authentic version.

        —N.L.M.